START STRONG WORKBOOK

A NEW BELIEVER'S GUIDE TO CHRISTIANITY

KRISAN MAROTTA

EZRA'S PATH
PUBLISHING

First Edition January 2026

Ezra's Path Publishing, Charlottesville, VA

ISBN: 979-8-9997508-4-6 (paperback)

CONTENTS

BEFORE YOU BEGIN

Welcome. If you're new to the faith or helping someone who is, you are in the right place. This workbook is designed to walk with you through *Start Strong: A New Believer's Guide to Christianity*. Think of it as a steady companion that helps you slow down, look closely at Scripture, and respond to what you learn.

You do not need special training to use this workbook. Bring a Bible, a pen, and a willingness to learn. If you have a friend or small group to join you, even better.

HOW TO USE THIS WORKBOOK

- **Read the chapter in the book first.** Then open the matching chapter here.
- **Keep a Bible open.** In the Start Strong book, I quote from the *English Standard Version*, but use any translation you understand.
- **Move at your own pace.** You can work through a chapter in one sitting or spread it over several shorter intervals during the week. Whatever fits your schedule.

- **Pray before and after.** Ask God to teach you and to help you respond with faith.
- **Write as if you are talking to a trusted friend.** The goal is honesty, not perfection. No one has to see it but you.

WHAT IS IN EACH CHAPTER

Review Questions

These questions reinforce the key themes, ideas, and terms from the chapter. They help you check your understanding and notice what matters most. Answer in your own words. If you are working with a group, talk through your answers and look at the verses together.

See for Yourself

Here you will study the same Bible passages listed in the book under "See for Yourself." Read them slowly. Mark what you learn about God, about people, and about faith. If a verse is hard to understand, note your question(s) and keep going. Understanding grows with practice.

Reflection Question

This is the same reflection question from the book. It is meant to nudge truth from your head into your heart. Take your time. Be specific. If you are in a group, listen well to others and keep the conversation gracious and grounded in Scripture.

Journal Prompts

These prompts help you apply what you learned to real life. Some will invite repentance, others will stir hope, and others will guide you to pray. Use the space to write, sketch, outline a next step, or draft a simple prayer.

SUGGESTED RHYTHM

- **Day 1:** Read the book chapter.
- **Day 2:** Do the review questions.
- **Day 3:** Study the "See for Yourself" passages.
- **Day 4-6:** Answer the reflection question or some of the journal prompts.

Adjust as needed. The aim is clarity and understanding.

TIPS FOR GROUPS

Open the Bible together. Read and study the listed passages before you discuss them with your group.

Stay curious and kind. Ask good questions and listen carefully.

Keep the main thing the main thing. Let Scripture lead; avoid speculation.

Pray for one another.

You'll find a free list of small group discussion questions at startstrongbook.org.

WHAT TO EXPECT

You will meet the same themes again and again: who God is, why the cross matters, what saving faith looks like, why trials cause growth, how love acts, and why perseverance matters. Repetition is a gift. Each pass adds clarity and confidence.

Getting stuck does not mean you are failing. It means you are learning. Bring your questions to Scripture, to prayer, and to another trusted believer. God is patient with learners.

A FINAL WORD

You do not need to be perfect to begin. You only need to be willing. Open your Bible. Ask good questions. Tell the truth in your journal. Take small, honest steps of obedience.

Over time you will see what countless believers have found: God's Word is clear, trustworthy, and life-giving. Let's start strong together.

SIN

THE PROBLEM WE CAN'T IGNORE

1. What is the main problem the Bible concentrates on?

_____

_____

_____

_____

_____

2. How is sin like a cracked mirror?

_____

_____

_____

_____

_____

3. Define repentance. Why is it more than just feeling sorry?

_____

_____

_____

_____

_____

4. What is entropy, and how does it explain sin?

_____

_____

_____

_____

_____

5. According to Romans 6:23, what are the "wages of sin" and what is God's free gift?

_____

_____

_____

_____

_____

6. How do the effects of sin spread beyond the individual who commits it?

_____

_____

_____

_____

_____

7. Define "eternal life" in your own words.

_____

_____

_____

_____

_____

8. What are three lies that keep people from repenting?

_____

_____

_____

_____

_____

9. What does the party boat on the waterfall analogy illustrate about sin and repentance?

_____

_____

_____

_____

_____

10. Why can't we fix our sin by ourselves? What do we need instead?

_____

_____

_____

_____

_____

~

SEE FOR YOURSELF

Romans 6:15–7:6

_____

_____

_____

Romans 8:12–25

_____

_____

_____

_____

_____

1 John 1:5–10

_____

_____

_____

_____

_____

Ephesians 2:1–10

_____

_____

_____

_____

_____

REFLECTION

If you knew that some of your habitual choices were quietly eroding your life and relationships, what first step would you take to confront and change them? What keeps you from taking that step?

_____

_____

_____

_____

_____

∼

JOURNAL PROMPTS

Sin as a Distortion: Write about a time when you realized your perspective on a situation, a person, or even God was distorted. How might sin have played a role in that?

_____

_____

_____

_____

_____

_____

_____

Repentance: Think of a moment when you realized you were going the wrong way in life (big or small). What helped you decide to turn around?

_____

_____

_____

_____

_____

_____

_____

Entropy: Where have you seen the unraveling of sin and death in your own life? How does that influence your understanding of needing God's help?

_____

_____

_____

_____

_____

_____

_____

The Ripple Effect: Sin spreads like ripples in a pond. Reflect on a time when someone's actions (yours or someone else's) hurt more than one person. What did that experience teach you?

_____

_____

_____

_____

_____

_____

_____

Hope Beyond the Falls: Imagine what life would be like without fear, guilt, or brokenness. How does that vision encourage you to trust Jesus today?

_____

_____

_____

_____

_____

_____

_____

GUILT

WHY GOOD INTENTIONS ARE NOT ENOUGH

1. In the courtroom illustration, why don't regret or remorse change the guilty verdict?

_____

_____

_____

_____

_____

2. What are the two devastating consequences of sin?

_____

_____

_____

_____

_____

3. What is a "broken chooser" and why can't we fix it?

_____

_____

_____

_____

_____

4. Why is it not enough to simply "try harder" or "make better choices?"

_____

_____

_____

_____

_____

5. What is God's wrath and how is it different from human anger?

_____

_____

_____

_____

_____

6. What three claims does Paul make in Romans 1:18–32?

_____

_____

_____

_____

_____

7. Why can't good deeds solve our guilt?

_____

_____

_____

_____

_____

8. Define justification in your own words.

_____

_____

_____

_____

_____

9. How is justification like having a billion-dollar debt paid for you?

_____

_____

_____

_____

_____

10. What is one way trusting Jesus' payment for your guilt could change how you live, based on the chapter?

_____

_____

_____

_____

_____

∽

SEE FOR YOURSELF

Romans 1:16–32

_____

_____

_____

Romans 3:1–31

_____
_____
_____
_____
_____

Galatians 3:1–14

_____
_____
_____
_____
_____

Psalm 51

_____
_____
_____
_____
_____

REFLECTION

Since guilt is an objective debt that must somehow be settled, who or what are you counting on to pay it, and on what basis do you trust that solution?

_____

_____

_____

_____

_____

∽

JOURNAL PROMPTS

Chains of Guilt: Write about a time you felt stuck in guilt or a bad habit, even when you wanted to change. How does knowing Jesus paid your debt change your thinking?

_____

_____

_____

_____

_____

_____

_____

_____

The Broken Chooser: Think of a time you chose something selfish over what was right. What did it teach you?

_____

_____

_____

_____

_____

_____

_____

Facing the Verdict: Reflect on a time when you tried to make amends for something wrong you did. How might understanding the cross change how you handle guilt?

_____

_____

_____

_____

_____

_____

_____

Sin's Takeover: Where have you seen sin mess up your life or someone else's? How does Jesus' rescue give you hope in that situation?

_____

_____

_____

_____

_____

_____

_____

_____

Freedom in Justification: Imagine walking out of a courtroom free because someone else paid your debt. How would that freedom affect your day-to-day life?

_____

_____

_____

_____

_____

_____

_____

_____

3

___

THE CROSS

WHY JESUS HAD TO DIE

1. How is our sin like a debt and what did Jesus do about it?

___

___

___

___

___

2. Define total depravity and how the yeast analogy explains it.

___

___

___

___

___

3. Why is sin a personal betrayal of God, not just breaking rules?

_____

_____

_____

_____

_____

4. How does viewing God as the faithful husband and us as the adulterous wife explain our situation?

_____

_____

_____

_____

_____

5. According to Colossians 2:13–14, what did God do with our record of debt?

_____

_____

_____

_____

_____

6. Why couldn't God forgive us without Jesus' death?

_____

_____

_____

_____

_____

7. Define atonement in your own words. What makes it a legal idea?

_____

_____

_____

_____

_____

8. What is a ransom, who needs it, and who sets the price?

_____

_____

_____

_____

_____

9. How do substitution and satisfaction describe Jesus' atoning sacrifice?

_____

_____

_____

_____

_____

10. Why isn't everyone automatically saved by Jesus' death?

_____

_____

_____

_____

_____

∽

SEE FOR YOURSELF

Isaiah 53:7–12

_____

_____

_____

_____

_____

Colossians 2:4–15

_____

_____

_____

_____

_____

John 3:16–21

_____

_____

_____

_____

_____

Hebrews 9:11–28

_____

_____

_____

_____

_____

REFLECTION

If someone truly absorbed the full cost of every wrong you've ever done, leaving you nothing to repay, how might that alter the way you view both your past failures and your future choices?

_____

_____

_____

_____

_____

~

JOURNAL PROMPTS

A Crushing Debt: Write about a time you felt overwhelmed by a mistake or problem you couldn't fix. How does Jesus paying your sin-debt change how you see that?

_____

_____

_____

_____

_____

_____

_____

Total Depravity: Think of a time you noticed sin affecting your thoughts or actions, even when you didn't want it to. How does knowing Jesus took that sin help you?

_____

_____

_____

_____

_____

_____

_____

The Faithful Husband: Reflect on a time you chose something (like comfort or approval) over trusting God. What were the consequences and what did you learn?

_____

_____

_____

_____

_____

_____

_____

Justice and Mercy: Write about a situation where you've seen justice and mercy together (in your life or someone else's). How does the cross make that real for you?

_____

_____

_____

_____

_____

_____

_____

Grace That Amazes: Imagine what your life might be like without that grace. How does knowing God chose to save you encourage you today?

_____

_____

_____

_____

_____

_____

_____

4

FAITH

WHAT IT MEANS TO TRUST JESUS

1. According to Ephesians 2:8–9, how are we saved, and why can't we boast about it?

_____

_____

_____

_____

_____

2. What's one thing saving faith is not? Pick one misconception and explain it in your own words.

_____

_____

_____

3. Summarize the lifeguard/hospital analogy in your own words.

_____

_____

_____

_____

_____

4. What does the "R" in R.E.A.L. faith stand for and what does it involve?

_____

_____

_____

_____

_____

5. Why can't we save ourselves according to the "E" in R.E.A.L. faith?

_____

_____

_____

_____

_____

6. What does the "A" in R.E.A.L. faith mean about how we view salvation?

_____

_____

_____

_____

_____

7. What does it mean to "Lean on Jesus alone" based on the "L" in R.E.A.L. faith?

_____

_____

_____

_____

_____

8. Explain why Paul and James do _not_ contradict each other about faith and works.

_____

_____

_____

_____

_____

9. How does Abraham's story with Isaac show R.E.A.L. faith in action?

_____

_____

_____

_____

_____

10. What's one way R.E.A.L. faith could change how you live, even if you still mess up?

_____

_____

_____

_____

_____

~

SEE FOR YOURSELF

Matthew 5:1–16

_____

_____

_____

James 2:14–26

_____

_____

_____

_____

_____

Galatians 2:11–21

_____

_____

_____

_____

_____

Romans 4:1–25

_____

_____

_____

_____

_____

REFLECTION

What does your lifestyle (what you celebrate, worry about, and sacrifice for) suggest about what you trust to secure your future, and how confident are you it can truly hold firm?

_____

_____

_____

_____

_____

~

JOURNAL PROMPTS

From Belief to Trust: Where have you treated "faith" like optimism or positive thinking? How does trusting Jesus change your outlook?

_____

_____

_____

_____

_____

_____

_____

R.E.A.L. Check-In: Which of the four convictions (Recognize, Embrace, Accept, Lean) comes hardest for you and why?

_____

_____

_____

_____

_____

_____

_____

Grace, Not Entitlement: Describe a moment you expected God to "owe" you. How does accepting grace as a gift reshape your attitude and thinking?

_____

_____

_____

_____

_____

_____

_____

Faith That Moves: Think of the firefighter image. What's one area where your choices proved you trust Jesus?

_____

_____

_____

_____

_____

_____

_____

Direction Over Perfection: What's one area where you still struggle to make good choices? Write a short prayer of grief, repentance, and hope, asking God to keep drawing you back to him.

_____

_____

_____

_____

_____

_____

_____

5

A NEW WAY OF SEEING

GOD AT THE CENTER

1. In the emancipation illustration, what changed when the messenger said, "You're free," and how does that compare to new believers?

_____

_____

_____

_____

_____

2. What is a worldview, and how does it compare to contact lenses?

_____

_____

_____

3. What is the Copernican shift of saving faith, and how does it re-center your perspective?

_____

_____

_____

_____

_____

4. How does a "self-at-the-center" perspective affect our attitude toward God and other people?

_____

_____

_____

_____

_____

5. How do Jesus' two greatest commandments flow logically from a God-centered reality?

_____

_____

_____

_____

_____

6. Summarize the playground analogy. What truth does it highlight?

_____

_____

_____

_____

_____

7. What does love mean in biblical terms: feeling or action? Explain.

_____

_____

_____

_____

_____

8. What's the "Golden Rule" and how does it reflect reality?

_____

_____

_____

_____

_____

9. How does Christian love differ from natural kindness?

_____

_____

_____

_____

_____

10. Why does Jesus say that loving even our enemies shows we are his disciples?

_____

_____

_____

_____

_____

~

SEE FOR YOURSELF

Philippians 2:5–11

_____

_____

_____

_____

_____

Matthew 7:12–29

_____

_____

_____

_____

_____

Luke 20:25–37

_____

_____

_____

_____

_____

Matthew 22:34–40

_____

_____

_____

_____

_____

REFLECTION

When everyday choices put your needs in conflict with someone else's, what guides your actions? How might that reveal who (or what) sits at the center of your world?

_____

_____

_____

_____

_____

∾

JOURNAL PROMPTS

A New View: Write about a time something shifted your perspective (big or small). How might seeing God at the center change how you view your life now?

_____

_____

_____

_____

_____

_____

_____

Equal Ground: Think of someone you've judged or looked down on. What would it look like to treat them as equals?

_____

_____

_____

_____

_____

_____

_____

Love in Action: Reflect on a time you helped someone (or didn't) when they needed it. What did you learn from that?

_____

_____

_____

_____

_____

_____

_____

The Golden Rule: Write about a time someone wronged you. If you were the one who had done the hurting, how would you want them to treat you? How could you show that to them now?

_____

_____

_____

_____

_____

_____

_____

_____

Equal Planets: Think of someone in your life you find hard to connect with. How could seeing them as a fellow sinner in need of grace change how you treat them?

_____

_____

_____

_____

_____

_____

_____

_____

6

THE CHURCH

FINDING YOUR NEW FAMILY

1. Why does equality before God lead to a special love for fellow believers? Give the biblical basis.

_____

_____

_____

_____

_____

2. Summarize the stadium/orange scarf picture. What truth does it teach?

_____

_____

_____

3. What did Jesus mean by "whoever receives you receives me?"

_____

_____

_____

_____

_____

4. How does welcoming ordinary believers (even with a "cup of cold water") honor Jesus? Explain in your own words.

_____

_____

_____

_____

_____

5. Summarize Jesus' new commandment. What is new about it?

_____

_____

_____

_____

_____

6. Why does Paul link genuine faith with visible love for believers? How does that help us "see" faith?

_____

_____

_____

_____

_____

7. Our attitude toward believers reveals our relationship to God. What are the warning signs?

_____

_____

_____

_____

_____

8. How does allegiance to Jesus transcend differences like race, class, politics, or personality within the church?

_____

_____

_____

_____

_____

9. What everyday actions show we treat disciples as family rather than as mere acquaintances? Give two examples.

---

10. In your own words, explain why loving fellow believers is a mark of real discipleship.

~

SEE FOR YOURSELF

Matthew 10:40–42

John 13:1–20

_____

_____

_____

_____

_____

Galatians 5:25–6:5

_____

_____

_____

_____

_____

1 John 3:13–24

_____

_____

_____

_____

_____

REFLECTION

Observe a community you belong to or are exploring. How does the way its members care for one another confirm or contradict the values they profess? What can you learn from that?

_____

_____

_____

_____

_____

～

JOURNAL PROMPTS

Team Colors: Where have you spotted the "same orange scarf" in real life? How did you respond, or how might you behave differently next time?

_____

_____

_____

_____

_____

_____

_____

Cup of Cold Water: Identify ways you "receive" other disciples as family in your community and church.

_____

_____

_____

_____

_____

_____

_____

_____

Just as I Have Loved You: Choose one friend you could love like Christ. What would Christ-like love look like in that relationship?

_____

_____

_____

_____

_____

_____

_____

_____

Faith You Can See: If someone only heard stories about how you treat fellow believers, what would they conclude about your faith?

_____

_____

_____

_____

_____

_____

_____

_____

When Faith is Mocked: Where have you seen believers belittled for taking Jesus seriously? How might you handle that situation if and when you face it?

_____

_____

_____

_____

_____

_____

_____

_____

7

DAILY LIFE

WHAT FOLLOWING JESUS LOOKS LIKE

1. What are the three goals for living as a follower of Jesus?

_____

_____

_____

_____

_____

2. What does the phrase "Jesus is Lord" mean?

_____

_____

_____

_____

_____

3. Why is confessing "Jesus is Lord" the mark of a believer?

_____

_____

_____

_____

_____

4. Why are spiritual experiences and religious activities not a mark of true belief?

_____

_____

_____

_____

_____

5. Why is the fear of the Lord the beginning of wisdom?

_____

_____

_____

_____

_____

6. Explain two wrong ways to fear God.

_____

_____

_____

_____

_____

7. Why does Jesus say to fear God more than people?

_____

_____

_____

_____

_____

8. What does it mean to "stand firm," and what's the battle about?

_____

_____

_____

_____

_____

9. Define "persevering in faith" in your own words.

_____

_____

_____

_____

_____

10. What's one way staying "awake" spiritually could change how you handle daily distractions?

_____

_____

_____

_____

_____

∼

SEE FOR YOURSELF

1 Corinthians 12:1–3

_____

_____

_____

_____

_____

1 Peter 5:6–14

_____

_____

_____

_____

_____

Ephesians 6:10–24

_____

_____

_____

_____

_____

Proverbs 1:7–9

_____

_____

_____

_____

_____

REFLECTION

Who or what do you recognize (consciously or unconsciously) as the highest authority in your life? How is that allegiance shaping your everyday decisions and long-term direction?

_____

_____

_____

_____

_____

~

JOURNAL PROMPTS

Say It: Write about a time you had to choose to stand up for what you believe. What did you learn?

_____

_____

_____

_____

_____

_____

_____

_____

Mean It: Think of a time where you cared more about what God thought than what others thought. What happened and what did you learn?

_____

_____

_____

_____

_____

_____

_____

_____

Keep It: Reflect on a tough time when you felt pulled off course. How did you handle it and what did you learn from it?

_____

_____

_____

_____

_____

_____

_____

_____

Stay Awake: Write about something (like school, friends, or fun) that pulls your focus from God. What helps you "stay awake?"

_____

_____

_____

_____

_____

_____

_____

_____

The Real Battle: Think of a struggle you're facing now. How could understanding the bigger story help you stand firm?

_____

_____

_____

_____

_____

_____

_____

_____

8

TRIALS

HOW GOD USES HARD TIMES

1. What is a "trial" and what do trials test?

_____

_____

_____

_____

_____

2. How does the refining gold analogy illustrate how God uses trials in our lives?

_____

_____

_____

_____

_____

3. What is the key question every trial challenges you to ask?

_____

_____

_____

_____

_____

4. What does God test in trials, and what does he not test?

_____

_____

_____

_____

_____

5. Why can we have joy in trials?

_____

_____

_____

_____

_____

6. How does the soccer team story illustrate a trial's purpose and results?

_____

_____

_____

_____

_____

7. What does Peter's denial and restoration teach about trials?

_____

_____

_____

_____

8. Why are trials part of God's design, not anomalies?

_____

_____

_____

_____

9. What's the war we're in, and how do we "win" it?

_____

_____

_____

_____

_____

10. What confidence do past trials give you today and how do they help you trust God in a current struggle?

_____

_____

_____

_____

_____

∾

SEE FOR YOURSELF

1 Peter 1:1–13

_____

_____

_____

_____

_____

James 1:1–8

_____

_____

_____

_____

_____

Isaiah 43:1–3

_____

_____

_____

_____

Hebrews 12:5–11

_____

_____

_____

_____

REFLECTION

Think about a hard trial you faced. What did you learn from it?

_____

_____

_____

_____

_____

~

JOURNAL PROMPTS

Refined Faith: Write about a tough time that felt like you were "tested by fire." Looking back, can you see ways it made your trust in God stronger?

_____

_____

_____

_____

_____

_____

_____

Proving Ground: Think of a moment when you had to choose between an easy way out and trusting God. How did that choice show what you really believe?

_____

_____

_____

_____

_____

_____

_____

Joy in the Struggle: Reflect on a current or past hardship. How did you find joy in it?

_____

_____

_____

_____

_____

_____

_____

Stumbling Forward: Write about a time you felt far from God. How does understanding the purpose of trials encourage you to keep going?

_____

_____

_____

_____

_____

_____

_____

_____

Maturing Hope: Think of a challenge that taught you something about yourself or God. How might that lesson help you face the next challenge?

_____

_____

_____

_____

_____

_____

_____

_____

9

HOLINESS

LEARNING TO DESIRE WHAT'S GOOD

1. What common thread lies underneath our toughest temptations, and what key question does it force us to ask?

_____

_____

_____

_____

_____

2. In 1 Thessalonians 4:3, what does Paul say is God's will, and how does that frame the rest of his guidance?

_____

_____

_____

3. Explain the two main ideas of holiness in your own words.

_____

_____

_____

_____

_____

4. What's wrong with the "sin-meter" way of measuring growth?

_____

_____

_____

_____

_____

5. Explain sanctification in your own words.

_____

_____

_____

_____

_____

6. Why is holiness about belonging, and how does that belonging reshape our desires and choices?

_____

_____

_____

_____

_____

7. What's the difference between God's universal boundaries and individual boundaries, and why do we need both?

_____

_____

_____

_____

_____

8. What does "persistent indifference to sin" in contrast to "failures with repentance" reveal about our faith?

_____

_____

_____

_____

_____

9. Why is lasting change impossible by sheer willpower, and on whom do we depend?

_____

_____

_____

_____

_____

10. Is desire itself sinful? If not, what makes desires wrong?

_____

_____

_____

_____

_____

~

SEE FOR YOURSELF

Galatians 5:13–24

_____

_____

_____

_____

_____

1 Corinthians 6:9–20

_____

_____

_____

_____

_____

Romans 11:33–12:3

_____

_____

_____

_____

_____

1 Peter 2:1–10

_____

_____

_____

_____

_____

REFLECTION

When a strong desire tugs at you, what principle or authority do you consult before acting? Is that desire truly leading you toward the life you want?

_____

_____

_____

_____

_____

~

JOURNAL PROMPTS

Behaving Before Belonging: Write about a time you tried to track your growth with an internal "meter." How did it work? What did you learn?

_____

_____

_____

_____

_____

_____

_____

Desire Crossroads: Name one desire that tugs you in the wrong direction. What would choosing what God wants look like in that situation?

_____

_____

_____

_____

_____

_____

_____

Set Apart, Right Here: Identify one universal boundary and one personal boundary in your current season. How does each help you live like someone who belongs to God?

_____

_____

_____

_____

_____

_____

_____

When I Can't Change Myself: Think of a struggle where you feel stuck. What encourages you to persevere in the midst of it? Who can you turn to for support?

_____

_____

_____

_____

_____

_____

_____

Direction Over Perfection: Where have you shown repentance after failing? How does that pattern reassure you about God's work in you?

_____

_____

_____

_____

_____

_____

_____

10

SEX

TRUSTING GOD WITH DESIRE

1. According to 1 Thessalonians 4:3, what is God's will for your life?

_____

_____

_____

_____

_____

2. In your own words, summarize God's design for sexuality.

_____

_____

_____

_____

_____

3. Why is sex never "just physical?" What does it express inside marriage?

_____

_____

_____

_____

_____

4. Name two examples of sexual immorality the Bible says to avoid.

_____

_____

_____

_____

_____

5. What does it mean to "control your body in holiness and honor" (1 Thessalonians 4:4)?

_____

_____

_____

_____

_____

6. Why can something consensual still be harmful?

_____

_____

_____

_____

_____

7. List some examples of the difference between living by desire and living God's way.

_____

_____

_____

_____

_____

8. List some ways that handling sexuality can be a test of faith.

_____

_____

_____

_____

9. What should you do if you've messed up sexually?

_____

_____

_____

_____

_____

10. When faced with strong desires, what key question of trust should you ask yourself?

_____

_____

_____

_____

_____

~

SEE FOR YOURSELF

1 Thessalonians 4:1–12

_____

_____

_____

_____

_____

Genesis 2

_____

_____

_____

_____

_____

Matthew 5:27–30

_____

_____

_____

_____

_____

Proverbs 5:15–20

_____

_____

_____

_____

_____

REFLECTION

Where do you feel the biggest tension between God's design for sexuality and today's cultural norms? How do you navigate that?

_____

_____

_____

_____

_____

∼

JOURNAL PROMPTS

Set Apart: Write about a time you felt different because of your faith. What did you learn from that experience?

_____

_____

_____

_____

_____

_____

_____

_____

God's Design: Compare a message you've heard about sex and marriage from your culture with God's plan for sex and marriage.

_____

_____

_____

_____

_____

_____

_____

_____

Honor Others: Think of someone you are dating, might marry, or are married to. What would it look like to honor that person in your relationship?

_____

_____

_____

_____

_____

_____

_____

_____

Facing Failure: If your private life were suddenly public, what would you want to be true of it? How might you change now to make that true?

_____

_____

_____

_____

_____

_____

_____

Trusting Him: Think of a situation where God's way feels too hard. What would it look like to trust his design instead of your own? Who could support you in that choice?

_____

_____

_____

_____

_____

_____

_____

11

WORK

SERVING GOD IN DAILY LIFE

1. What does 1 Thessalonians 4:11–12 say about how believers should work?

_____

_____

_____

_____

_____

2. Why did some Thessalonians stop working? What was wrong with stopping?

_____

_____

_____

3. In your own words, how is work a daily act of loving your neighbor? Give examples.

_____

_____

_____

_____

_____

4. What does "aspire to live quietly" mean (1 Thessalonians 4:11)? How does it relate to trusting God with both opportunities and outcomes?

_____

_____

_____

_____

_____

5. How are God's boundaries for work both universal and personal?

_____

_____

_____

_____

_____

6. What happens when we step outside God's boundaries?

_____

_____

_____

_____

_____

7. Explain the difference between living quietly and living for impact.

_____

_____

_____

_____

_____

8. What's wrong with refusing to work when you're able?

_____

_____

_____

_____

9. What can we learn from Paul's choice to make tents to support his teaching?

_____

_____

_____

_____

_____

10. Compare the common view of work with the biblical view of work.

_____

_____

_____

_____

_____

∽

SEE FOR YOURSELF

1 Thessalonians 4:9–12

_____

_____

_____

2 Thessalonians 3:1–18

_____

_____

_____

_____

_____

Proverbs 6:6–11, 21:25, 24:30–34

_____

_____

_____

_____

_____

Colossians 3:18–4:1

_____

_____

_____

_____

REFLECTION

How does viewing work as part of loving your neighbor challenge or affirm your current view of your job and daily responsibilities?

_____

_____

_____

_____

_____

∾

JOURNAL PROMPTS

Loving Through Work: Write about a time your work (a chore, job, or favor) helped someone. How could seeing it as love change how you approach work next time?

_____

_____

_____

_____

_____

_____

_____

Quiet Faithfulness: Think of a time you felt pressure to do more or be noticed. How might trusting God free you to be content?

_____

_____

_____

_____

_____

_____

_____

Boundaries and Trust: Reflect on one of God's boundaries you are tempted to ignore. What would trusting God's wisdom look like there?

_____

_____

_____

_____

_____

_____

_____

Stumbling Block: Write about a time you avoided responsibility or chased recognition. What did you learn from that experience?

_____

_____

_____

_____

_____

_____

_____

_____

Simple Obedience: Think of a small task you do regularly (homework, chores, etc.). How could doing it faithfully show love and trust in God?

_____

_____

_____

_____

_____

_____

_____

12

MONEY

TRUSTING GOD, NOT WEALTH

1. What verses from Jesus frame this chapter? Explain the main idea in your own words.

_____

_____

_____

_____

_____

2. What is the problem with money? Include one Scripture.

_____

_____

_____

_____

_____

3. Explain how wealth acts like a master in daily life.

_____

_____

_____

_____

_____

4. Give two examples of how serving wealth can "set the rules" for your time and relationships.

_____

_____

_____

_____

_____

5. Explain what Jesus means about loving one master and hating the other.

_____

_____

_____

_____

_____

6. Summarize the "two bosses" example. How does that picture explain why we can't serve both God and money?

_____

_____

_____

_____

_____

7. Does Scripture condemn wealth itself? What does it condemn, and why?

_____

_____

_____

_____

_____

8. Explain why the decisive question is not, "How much can I earn?" but "Who do I trust?"

_____

_____

_____

_____

_____

9. Describe one way clinging to God's promises might require loosening your grip on possessions.

_____

_____

_____

_____

_____

10. Compare and contrast what God says about wealth with what the world says about wealth.

_____

_____

_____

_____

_____

∾

SEE FOR YOURSELF

Deuteronomy 8:11–18

_____

_____

_____

Matthew 19:16–24

_____

_____

_____

_____

_____

Luke 12:15–21

_____

_____

_____

_____

_____

Proverbs 3:9–10; 11:24–28; 30:7–9

_____

_____

_____

_____

_____

REFLECTION

When a financial opportunity conflicts with your core princi-
ples, which side wins? What does that choice reveal about what
you ultimately trust?

~

JOURNAL PROMPTS

The Invisible Master: Write about a time money promised
"security" if you obeyed, and threatened "anxiety" if you didn't.
Did it fulfill its promise?

Playing for Both Teams: Describe a situation (real or imagined) where serving God's priorities would cost you financially, socially, or professionally.

_____

_____

_____

_____

_____

_____

_____

_____

Giver or Gifts: Make two short lists: (1) the "gifts" you tend to cling to (savings goals, lifestyle, status items), and (2) the promises of God you want to cling to instead.

_____

_____

_____

_____

_____

_____

_____

_____

Loosen Your Grip: Write about one possession, expense, or habit you should hold more loosely. What small act of generosity or contentment would be a faithful next step?

_____

_____

_____

_____

_____

_____

_____

_____

House Rules: If God's "household rules" were posted on your refrigerator, what would change in how you spend, save, and give?

_____

_____

_____

_____

_____

_____

_____

_____

13

THE HOLY SPIRIT

YOUR HELPER IN THE CHRISTIAN LIFE

1. What does Ephesians 1:13–14 say the Holy Spirit?

_____

_____

_____

_____

_____

2. How did the promise of the Spirit come true at Pentecost?

_____

_____

_____

_____

_____

3. Explain in your own words what the seal of the Spirit means.

_____

_____

_____

_____

_____

4. Why is the Spirit called a pledge of our inheritance in Ephesians 1:13–14?

_____

_____

_____

_____

_____

5. Explain in your own words why Jesus compares the Spirit to wind in John 3.

_____

_____

_____

_____

_____

6. How does the Spirit make us "born again" (John 3)?

_____

_____

_____

_____

_____

7. Explain Paul's analogy of the body for spiritual gifts in 1 Corinthians 12.

_____

_____

_____

_____

_____

8. What's the purpose of spiritual gifts?

_____

_____

_____

_____

9. How can we find and use our gifts or roles?

_____

_____

_____

_____

_____

10. Compare and contrast different views of spiritual gifts.

_____

_____

_____

_____

_____

∽

SEE FOR YOURSELF

Ephesians 1:13–23

_____

_____

_____

_____

_____

John 3:1–13

_____

_____

_____

_____

_____

1 Corinthians 12

_____

_____

_____

_____

_____

Acts 2:1–4

_____

_____

_____

_____

_____

REFLECTION

Where have you noticed a practical need in your church, work-place, neighborhood, or circle of friends, and what first step could you take to help fill it?

_____

_____

_____

_____

_____

~

Journal Prompts

Sealed by God: Write about a time you felt sure (or unsure) of God's claim on your life. How does understanding the Spirit's role encourage you?

_____

_____

_____

_____

_____

_____

_____

Wind of Change: Think of a change in your life you didn't expect. How might the Spirit have been working in that change?

_____

_____

_____

_____

_____

_____

_____

Born Again: Reflect on a time you wanted to start over in some way. How could trusting the Spirit's work give you hope for that now?

_____

_____

_____

_____

_____

_____

_____

Part of the Body: Write about a time you felt connected to or disconnected from other believers. How could serving with them build that bond?

_____

_____

_____

_____

_____

_____

_____

_____

Serving With Grace: Think of a way you helped someone lately (or could). How might the Spirit use that situation to show God's love?

_____

_____

_____

_____

_____

_____

_____

_____

14

HOPE

HOLDING ON UNTIL THE END

1. What does Jesus promise in Matthew 7:7 about asking, seeking, and knocking?

_____

_____

_____

_____

_____

2. How does the good father picture illustrate what Jesus means by ask, seek, knock?

_____

_____

_____

3. What do we deserve because of our sin? What does God give instead?

_____

_____

_____

_____

_____

4. What is one thing God will always give when we ask?

_____

_____

_____

_____

5. Why might God say "no" to some prayers?

_____

_____

_____

_____

6. What is the role of doubt in the journey of faith?

_____

_____

_____

_____

_____

7. Describe the difference between our view and God's view of good gifts.

_____

_____

_____

_____

_____

8. Why do Paul and Jesus warn that Christ's return will be like a thief in the night, and how should believers respond?

_____

_____

_____

_____

_____

9. Why should we keep asking, seeking, and knocking no matter what?

_____

_____

_____

_____

_____

10. Explain the difference between biblical hope, wishful thinking, and optimism in your own words.

_____

_____

_____

_____

_____

~

SEE FOR YOURSELF

Romans 5:1–11

_____

_____

_____

Matthew 7:7–11

_____
_____
_____
_____
_____

1 Peter 1:1–13

_____
_____
_____
_____
_____

Romans 8:12–25

_____
_____
_____
_____
_____

REFLECTION

Do you struggle to believe God will answer your prayers? Why or why not?

_____

_____

_____

_____

_____

~

JOURNAL PROMPTS

God's Wisdom: Reflect on a time when God said no or made you wait, but it turned out better in the end. What did you learn?

_____

_____

_____

_____

_____

_____

_____

Our Sinfulness: Write about a moment when you felt guilty or unworthy because of a mistake. How does the hope of the gospel encourage you?

_____

_____

_____

_____

_____

_____

_____

God's Good Gifts: Write about a time when you wanted something, but God gave you something different that was better.

_____

_____

_____

_____

_____

_____

_____

Faith and Doubt: Think about a time when you doubted God's promises or felt like giving up. What got you through?

_____

_____

_____

_____

_____

_____

_____

_____

Persevering in Prayer: Write about a situation where you're waiting for an answer to prayer. What encourages you to persevere?

_____

_____

_____

_____

_____

_____

_____

_____

15

EIGHT TRUTHS TO REMEMBER

1. How does the superhero movie example illustrate the wrong way to apply the gospel?

_____

_____

_____

_____

_____

2. How does the prince in the fairy tale illustrate the right way to view the gospel?

_____

_____

_____

3. What does the gospel require? (Hint: It's not about earning something.)

_____

_____

_____

_____

_____

4. Explain the Holy Spirit's role in helping believers finish the race.

_____

_____

_____

_____

_____

5. List the eight truths in your own words.

_____

_____

_____

_____

_____

6. Describe one detour you struggle with. Why is it appealing, and how does one of the eight truths point you back to the path?

_____

_____

_____

_____

_____

7. Why don't we have the right to judge others?

_____

_____

_____

_____

_____

8. Imagine a friend who is discouraged. Which of the eight truths would you share first to encourage him or her?

_____

_____

_____

_____

_____

9. What is your "next faithful step," and which truth anchors it?

_____

_____

_____

_____

_____

10. What's one choice you've made lately that shows what you trust?

_____

_____

_____

_____

_____

~

SEE FOR YOURSELF

Colossians 1:13–23 (Truth #2)

_____

_____

_____

_____

_____

Romans 3:1–31 (Truth #3)

_____

_____

_____

_____

_____

Isaiah 40:12–31 (Truth #4 & #5)

_____

_____

_____

_____

_____

Romans 5:1–11 (Truth #5 & #7)

_____

_____

_____

_____

_____

Ephesians 4:11–16 (Truth #6)

_____

_____

_____

_____

_____

Galatians 5:16–26 (Truth #8)

_____

_____

_____

_____

_____

JOURNAL PROMPTS

Mile Marker: Picture your walk with Christ as a long-distance race. Where are you today (tired, steady or gaining strength)? Which one of the eight truths do you need most, and why?

_____

_____

_____

_____

_____

_____

_____

Truth Over Feelings: Describe a time when your feelings, fears, or circumstances shouted louder than your faith. Which truth from the chapter speaks directly to that moment?

_____

_____

_____

_____

_____

_____

_____

Finish-line Preview: Imagine looking back one year from now. How do you hope your life will be different?

_____

_____

_____

_____

_____

_____

_____

_____

Bring a Friend: Name one person you could encourage with these truths. Write a brief note you could actually send.

_____

_____

_____

_____

_____

_____

_____

_____

∾

FINAL THOUGHTS

Challenge: What did you learn from this book that challenged you most?

_____

_____

_____

_____

_____

_____

_____

Surprise: What did you learn from this book that surprised you most?

_____

_____

_____

_____

_____

_____

_____

Encouragement: What did you learn from this book that encouraged you most?

_____

_____

_____

_____

_____

_____

_____

_____

Prayer: What do you want to remember and pray about most?

_____

_____

_____

_____

_____

_____

_____

_____

Next: What do you want to learn next? Or what questions or ideas do you want to explore further?

_____

_____

_____

_____

_____

_____

_____

_____

_____

_____

_____

_____

_____

_____

A NOTE AT THE END

PLEASE REVIEW THIS BOOK!

Reviews help authors more than you think! If you were blessed by this book, please write a review on Amazon. Even if it's only a line or two, I would greatly appreciate it.

Scan this code to leave a review on Amazon:

And please tell a friend about *Start Strong*. A book in the right hands at the right time can change a life.

KEEP LEARNING

Wednesday in the Word is my podcast about what the Bible means and how we know. Each season covers a book of the Bible or a topical study. It's the same clear, thoughtful, and biblically grounded approach you've seen here, just in audio form.

Subscribe wherever you listen to your podcasts or visit WednesdayintheWord.com to listen and learn more.

READER AND LEADER EXTRAS

Whether you're reading on your own or leading a group, these tools are here to serve you.

All resources at krisan.com/startstrongbonus

Start Strong: A New Believer's Podcast: Each episode unpacks a key Bible passage from the "See for Yourself" list, explained clearly, applied practically. Build your faith with real understanding. Listen free on the *Wednesday in the Word with Krisan Marotta* podcast.

~

Free Discussion Questions: These questions help you reflect more deeply, spark meaningful conversation, and apply what you're learning to real life. Ideal for book clubs, small groups, mentoring, and discipling.

Free Leader Lesson Plans: This chapter-by-chapter guide is built for teaching, discussing, and applying the Scripture behind *Start Strong* in any classroom setting. Each plan includes Scripture, key themes, and open-ended questions.

Quizzes for Youth & Homeschoolers: Two quick, multiple-choice comprehension quizzes—one for Middle Grades (6–8) and one for High School (9–12)—to help students review what they've learned from *Start Strong* and identify what they might want to revisit.

Bulk Buying Discounts: If you're ordering for a church, campus ministry, homeschool co-op, or class, contact me and I'll help you figure out the best way to order for your group.

ABOUT THE AUTHOR

Krisan Marotta is the creator and host of Wednesday in the Word, the podcast about what the Bible means and how we know. Drawing on over forty years of Bible study and postgraduate work in biblical exegesis, she turns complex passages into clear, practical insight that empowers everyday believers to read Scripture for themselves. Krisan and her husband live in Charlottesville, Virginia, where she balances writing, podcasting, clog dancing, and delighting in the adventures of her grandchildren. Follow her books at krisan.com.